T0129638

THE PRACTICAL STRATEGIES SERIES
IN GIFTED EDUCATION

series editors
FRANCES A. KARNES & KRISTEN R. STEPHENS

The Challenges of Educating
the Gifted in Rural Areas

Joan D. Lewis, Ph.D.

Routledge
Taylor & Francis Group

NEW YORK AND LONDON

First published 2009 by Prufrock Press Inc.

Published 2021 by Routledge
605 Third Avenue, New York, NY 10017
2 Park Square, Milton Park, Abingdon, Oxon OX14 4RN

Routledge is an imprint of the Taylor & Francis Group, an informa business

ISBN 13: 978-1-59363-380-6 (pbk)

Contents

Series Preface   1

Acknowledgements   3

Introduction   5

Defining Rural   8

Challenges and Perspectives   10

Benefits and Accommodations   22

Adapting Traditional Gifted Education for Rural Settings   28

Conclusion   51

Resources   53

References   61

About the Author   67

The Practical Strategies Series in Gifted Education offers teachers, counselors, administrators, parents, and other interested parties up-to-date instructional techniques and information on a variety of issues pertinent to the field of gifted education. Each guide addresses a focused topic and is written by an individual with authority on the issue. Several guides have been published. Among the titles are:

- *Acceleration Strategies for Teaching Gifted Learners*
- *Curriculum Compacting: An Easy Start to Differentiating for High-Potential Students*
- *Enrichment Opportunities for Gifted Learners*
- *Independent Study for Gifted Learners*
- *Motivating Gifted Learners*
- *Questioning Strategies for Teaching the Gifted*
- *Social & Emotional Teaching Strategies*
- *Using Media & Technology with Gifted Students*

For a current listing of available guides within the series, please contact Prufrock Press at 800-998-2208 or visit http://www.prufrock.com.

Acknowledgements

Thank you to Thomas Godfrey for his assistance in all phases of assembling this volume. The sample rows from parallel menu activities for typical and gifted students developed by Stacey Gibbs were used with permission. Her willingness to share her work with others is gratefully appreciated.

Providing a high standard of education for our rural as well as urban students has been this country's intent, but often we have failed to achieve this goal. A number of factors have made guaranteeing educational equality for all students, regardless of location, more of a work-in-progress than a reality. The reasons for the failure of our resolve have been well documented, but increasingly evidence has accumulated that favors rural classroom innovations as opportunities for achieving educational success, despite apparent obstacles.

Awareness of rural education's ingenuity in accomplishing much with very little budgetary support for curricular improvement has begun to take root in the educational community. There are important reasons for this new focus on rural education. "More than 40% of all American schools are in rural areas and 30% of all students attend rural schools" (National Research Center on Rural Education Support [NRCRES], 2005, para. 2). "The poorest rural populations are in the poorest states [which are] least able to afford the cost of an adequate education" (Johnson & Strange, 2007, p. vi). These statistics highlight the need for paying attention to rural education. The links between low incomes and poverty, reduced level of education, and small towns/rural areas are even greater for families of minority groups (Colangelo, Assouline, & New, 1999). Even though states with the highest percentage of culturally diverse students must provide for "the highest percentage of public elementary students taking advantage of the federally funded free and reduced lunch program" (Colangelo et al., 1999, p. 44), some modest redirection of state resources could incentivize teaching innovation in and outside classrooms.

Rural education has gained respectful attention for a variety of reasons, despite the absence of uniform funding-allocation formulas among state legislatures. School enrollments have increased substantially in communities of 2,500 and under while larger communities have witnessed a decrease in students (Johnson & Strange, 2007). In fact, the 12 most populous states account for almost 50% of rural enrollees. The nation has denied proportionate financial support to small-town education in favor of urban or large suburban communities. Inequities of salary and benefits in smaller districts are slowly being addressed, but disparities still exist, especially in high-poverty regions (Johnson & Strange, 2007). "As rural America grows increasingly [culturally] diverse, the need for adequate resources and supportive policy environments to meet the needs of English Language Learner (ELL) students grows even more important" (Johnson & Strange, 2007, p. vi). More help nationally is being siphoned from rural use to the growing number of non-English-speaking young immigrants, due to their need to be assimilated culturally and vocationally.

Other obstacles need to be overcome. Student drop-out rates remain high in many cities and small towns alike. In rural areas, school consolidation continues to crowd single-building schools that often are the pride and social centers of small communities. The consolidation of schools continues despite research that concludes small schools serve their enrollees better than mergers—as verified by improved graduation rates, attendance, and achievement levels (Johnson & Strange, 2007).

Given these realities, it is only natural to ask how best to maintain a quality educational program in remote areas where funding is limited by lower population numbers, and recruiting experienced teachers (especially ones with specialized training) is problematic. Can resources be found to establish high-quality programs that meet the needs of all students, particularly high achievers? The content of this book aims to address these questions affirmatively and to identify and examine the components of a workable, successful collaboration among school administrators, teachers, students, parents, and other supporters from the community. The idea is to accomplish together what cannot be done separately.

Defining Rural

Just what constitutes rural is difficult to define and is becoming increasingly more complicated as the demographics of America evolve. Arnold, Biscoe, Farmer, Robertson, and Shapley (2007) have attempted to systematize the growing diversity by dispensing with terminology that seems vague. For years, even the federal government's many definitions of rural were inconsistent and frequently of little use, such as "not metropolitan." Arnold et al. describe six major categories of federal definitions (see Table 1); "all have been used in some way to better understand the challenges facing rural schools" (p. iii), including those with "reference to population density, geographic features, and levels of economic and industrial development" (p. iii). "Clearly defining what rural means has tangible implications for public policies and practices in education, from establishing resource needs to achieving the goals of No Child Left Behind in rural areas" (Arnold et al., 2007, p. iii).

In 2006, the National Center for Education Statistics (NCES), as a way of settling the debate about similarities and differences between regions, refined its definition to concentrate on what it calls the "urban-centric" dichotomy. The four

Table 1
Six Categories of Federal Definitions

Definitions of "rural" are based on the following criteria and/or used for the following purposes:
- U.S. Census Bureau: "geographic features, population, and as a residual" (p. iii)
- Metropolitan status codes: "relative to a core-based statistical area" (p. iii)
- Urban-rural continuum codes: "population and proximity to urban areas" (p. iv)
- Metro-centric locale codes: used "primarily for statistical procedures" (p. iv)
- Urban-centric locale codes: used to "improve the reliability and precision of local code assignment" (p. iv)
- Core-based statistical areas: "statistically defined geographic areas" (p. iv)

Note. From Arnold et al. (2007).

main terms used by NCES (city, suburban, town, and rural) are meant to call attention to the disparities between large and small, remote and densely settled, homogenous and heterogeneous. These distinctions are further subdivided into three groups each yielding another 12 distinct categories. "Town" and "rural," for instance, are separated, respectively, by their degrees of dense or sparse population with the application of categorical names (e.g., fringe, distant, or remote) to emphasize gradations of similarity or difference between each setting (Institute of Education Sciences [IES], n.d., para. 2). This novel classification forces planners to recognize "towns" inclusive of villages or hamlets and to contrast these diminutive entities with the various degrees of suburbanization. Rather than just relying on population numbers as in the past, the new terminology recognizes important differences between rural schools in isolated areas and those close to metropolitan centers. For the purposes of this publication, the NCES definition will be used.

Challenges and Perspectives

Children and adults differ in their mental acuity, learning styles, interests, motor skills, and life experiences, among many other factors. This diversity of learning readiness must be considered when preparing instruction regardless of students' age. Although rural learners benefit from less competition for teacher attention, they still vie for recognition of their unique capabilities. That need to be challenged academically frequently results in a lack of recognition, understanding, or interest from educators and community members alike. Academically talented students need the same status as athletically proficient individuals. Rural culture too often stresses motor over mental skills, resulting in the importance of academic competency and excellence being subordinate to performance in sports. Yet the potential for successfully meeting the learning needs of gifted individuals in rural schools is very high.

Students' Perspective

School Size and Homogeneity

Rural school districts labor under several apparent disadvantages. Most obviously, their enrollment is limited by low population density and concomitant remote locations. Related to these issues is the lack of diversity or the homogeneity of the student population. Furthermore, the smaller the school, the fewer number of gifted students at any one grade level or school-wide, and in the opinion of many educators, too few students to warrant specialized programs and services.

Gifted children, whether formally identified or not, are unlikely to receive the rigorous classroom work they need in order to learn at their appropriate challenge level (Gentry, 2006). Their educational needs often are overshadowed by the more pressing needs of federally mandated special education programs (Colangelo, Assouline, & New, 2001). Because of these federal regulations, focus is placed on low-achieving students rather than on their highly talented classmates. The No Child Left Behind Act (NCLB), with its focus on those not performing at grade level, is monopolizing instructional time with the consequence being a loss of attention to educational programs and services for gifted learners. Instead, programs that emphasize rote memorization and traditional curricular materials and practices are taking the forefront in order to prepare students for standardized tests. Such emphasis on testing has been widely discredited as being only marginally beneficial, especially for gifted students (Clark, 2008). An unintentional consequence of NCLB's mandate for annual yearly progress (AYP) measurement, with its focus on underperforming students, is that many educators are unaware as to how little growth gifted students all over the country may actually be making from year to year (see, for example, Clark, 2005; Gentry, 2006; Mendozo, 2006). In some cases, gifted students may actually be losing ground academically (Azzam, 2007/2008).

Career Planning

Small schools and communities afford limited job opportunities (Colangelo & Davis, 2003). Perhaps more than other gifted learners, rural youth need to know they can be anything they want. They need that permission—that there are many tantalizing careers that not only interest them but fit their abilities. This challenge can be offset by introducing job seekers to Internet resources where they can take virtual field trips to a wide range of work places independently or using planned instruction such as a WebQuest. A WebQuest is "an inquiry-oriented activity in which some or all of the information that learners interact with comes from resources on the Internet, optionally supplemented with videoconferencing" (Dodge, 1995, para. 2). Indeed, some students could develop their own WebQuests of various careers for other students to explore (Lewis & Clark, 2003).

A surprising number of residents in rural communities work in trades or professions of interest to students. These adults usually can be invited to speak informally at the invitation of instructors. Gifted students need guidance (academic, work-related, and psychological) when they become discouraged about their vocational prospects. Their aspirations for careers in science, performance arts, or entrepreneurship slip away unless encouraged by personal contact with enthusiastic role models. For example, Rob gave up his dream of being an aeronautical engineer after struggling with a difficult, uninspiring teacher of physics who knew little about his subject. Rob eventually settled for a career in business. He didn't enjoy this line of work, but it was something he could see himself doing in his small town. Stacy wanted to be an astronomer, but even with an enlightened family, couldn't decide how to pursue her dream and was unable to find others to counsel her. As a result, by seventh grade, she was talking about becoming a journalist and writing about astronomy. Being more the exception than the rule, Carl beat the odds and became an architect who works and travels worldwide. He tried to remain near home but was frustrated by a dull social life. His example personifies a fear among rural people that encouraging gifted students alienates them from their family upbringing; they eventually leave because there is no challenging work for them in their hometowns and no colleagues to feed their ever-questing minds. The social and emotional need these gifted learners have as children, to interact with peers of similar interest and ability, remains throughout their lives.

Peer Relations

Friendships may be more difficult to cultivate because gifted peers are few in sparsely populated areas. Gifted children need more mature friendships than other children of similar age (Gross, 2002). Typically all age groups seek out persons with similar intellects and needs. Building strong friendship bonds among gifted peers may not be easy, leading to possible isolation of the gifted child (Gross, 2002). Some gifted students will hide their abilities and deny their talents, in order to fit in with their age peers, while others flaunt their "giftedness" (Clark, 2008). Some aren't aware of how different they are. A key factor is developing an understanding of the social and emotional needs of gifted learners in addition to their academic needs. Informed parents and teachers can initiate long distance learning opportunities with other school districts and encourage using technology such as e-mail and Voice Over Internet Protocol (VoIP; i.e., Skype) to carry on conversations with distant friends from other schools.

Gifted students need intellectual peers to stave off the intellectual and social isolation many experience (Colangelo et al., 1999), not just occasionally but on a regular basis. To the extent possible, gifted learners need frequent opportunities to learn with like-ability peers. This may entail working with one or two students from different grade levels in areas of strength. Early finishers frequently are called upon to tutor slower classmates in the mistaken belief each will benefit. Gifted students are not always suitable tutors for other children, but the policy is widespread. Older gifted students (identified or not) can be role models for the younger ones, but not at the expense of their own learning time. A balance between helping others and a pursuit of personal challenges should be achieved to ensure that time is preserved for gifted learners to grow both academically and socially.

Attitudes and Obstacles

Gifted education often is seen as elitist (e.g., Clark, 2008; Colangelo & Davis, 2003; Davis & Rimm, 2004; Howley, Howley, & Pendarvis, 1995; Karnes & Stephens, 2008). Rural community citizens as well as educators may influence attitudes that hamper the implementation of special academic services. Schools may seem anti-intellectual (Howley et al., 1995), but few actively discourage high academic performance. The public mood may favor preparing farmers, loggers, and railroad workers to meet community needs as well as focus on sports rivalries. Special attention paid to the academically gifted frequently is overshadowed by these popular school and community activities.

Nevertheless, townspeople may support gifted education if they are helped to see its value to them and their community. One father of a gifted student and athlete told the teacher he was withdrawing his son from the gifted program because he was receiving undue attention. Thinking quickly, the teacher sorrowfully said she supposed his son would no longer be able to play football either given the recent newspaper article describing his son's athletic prowess on the football field. The father looked abashed and quietly assured the teacher his son would continue in both—he "got it."

Fewer students (including gifted ones) from rural areas attend college than those from more metropolitan areas—a discrepancy that has nearly tripled since 1960. Role models are needed who can motivate talented high schoolers and help them begin preparing for higher education. Families come to take pride in their sons and daughters who succeed in attending college, even when parents may never have considered this level of education for their children (Colangelo et al., 1999).

Transportation

Reliable transportation can be a major challenge in rural areas. Although some rural schools are isolated but have relatively compact service areas, such as on a small island in the Outer Banks or in a valley tucked between mountains in West Virginia, others serve students who must travel an hour each direction to school. The more schools consolidate, the greater the problem. The result for the students is they may have to adhere to a tight bus or parental work schedule that may discourage involvement in before- and after-school activities. Although not the best practice, some gifted programs compromise by only serving students during these times before and after school, thus potentially excluding those children who have difficult travel schedules.

Students' ability to use the local public library also may be severely curtailed due to transportation issues. To overcome this restriction, some teachers check out books for students to use in class. School library materials thus can be supplemented, despite what might still be a limited collection of books and other resources. In addition, students miss the opportunity to learn and practice library research skills unless librarians furnish direction through tutoring materials and can provide access to college-level databases and other resources. The Internet, if access is available, can provide students with a wide array of resource materials, thus helping to alleviate many of these issues.

Educators' Perspective

Instructional Materials and Resources

In rural areas, school systems still appear much as they did in the early 20th century. Building and classroom size reflect small enrollments, often less than a hundred total students in grades K–12. Equipment and room configurations look the same as they did in the 1950s. Textbooks are often more than 20 years old, especially in English, social studies, and history classes. Teachers sometimes teach subjects in which they are minimally qualified. School budgets are constrained by relatively sparse population so economizing is a watchword.

Although these factors suggest an antiquated approach to education, this isn't necessarily so. Federal and state programs have been instituted and expanded in the last decades. These have been guided by legislators mindful of their constituents' attitudes toward improving educational opportunities for their sons and daughters. Grants from government and private charitable organizations have resulted in facilities being upgraded, more qualified teachers being hired, and instructional materials being updated. An enlightened electorate has brought more rural locations into a national community of instruction and learning.

Scheduling

Remoteness, extreme commuting distance, and inadequate population bases influence rural school activity scheduling, class offerings, and both formal and informal learning opportunities. All of these challenges must be met to accommodate the community's students. One solution is to lengthen the school day by as much as an hour. Forty-five minute classes could be lengthened; an additional class could be inserted into the student's program; and collaboration can be encouraged between administrators, teachers, and students to expand options. A rural school must rely on cooperation, compromise, and comity.

Homeschooling, a practice that once was frowned on by professional educators, has flourished and gained respect since the late 1990s. Well-designed courses of instruction are available in virtually all mainstream subjects. Terrain barriers (e.g., mountains, rivers, lakes, oceans, deserts) that isolate small towns and villages geographically can now be spanned by electronic instruction, often discussed under the designation of "distance learning" (Lewis & Hafer, 2007). Courses that once were not offered due to low student enrollment now can be available to even one student who needs or desires instruction in a particular content area. Furthermore, many online courses are asynchronous, thus allowing students the flexibility to engage with the course content at times that are conducive to their schedule.

Attitudes and Perceptions

Many of the challenges in this section are not restricted to teachers in rural schools; however, the consequences are exacerbated in small schools because teaching candidates are fewer, and their exposure to innovative instructional theories and methods may be limited.

Anderson and Kleinsasser (as cited in Luhman & Fundis, 1989) described studies revealing that many rural teachers during the 1980s didn't think special programs for gifted students were important—a view that was not just restricted to rural America at the time. Some educators insist "those children" don't need extra help; they will make it on their own. On the other hand, there are educators who believe *all* children are gifted. This mistaken belief makes specialized instruction for gifted learners appear unnecessary.

However, gifted learners need teachers who task them with using their abilities productively—beyond other children's efforts. All children are valuable and need a quality education, but all are not gifted. Alternatively, specialized enrichment or acceleration may be denied to gifted learners because not all students would benefit. On the contrary, if the enrichment is tailored to fit all students then it isn't challenging enough for gifted learners. Clark (2008) points out accelerating curriculum delivery for everyone doesn't work either, because some students are left behind or gifted learners are impatiently waiting for some new intellectual or creative challenge. Another common misconception about acceleration is that children will be hurt socially, although the great preponderance of research discredits this enduring bias (e.g., Clark, 2008; Colangelo, Assouline, & Gross, 2004; Rogers, 1991). Acceleration has been shown to be an effective strategy for delivering advanced content to gifted students in their skill areas (Colangelo et al., 2004). It can be a practical adaptation to help gifted students in rural schools to increase their achievement in areas of strength (Howley, 2002). Howley specified that following certain guidelines increases the likelihood of success across several acceleration methods.

The movement to include students with disabilities in regular classes is based on the belief that this placement is the least restrictive learning environment and socialization opportunity for these students (Friend, 2008). By extension, many people erroneously believe the same is true for gifted learners. Unlike other students, these children benefit both socially and academically from being grouped with their academic peers at least part of the time (see Clark, 2008; Davis & Rimm, 2004; Kulik, 1992). Despite considerable research on this topic, there is a strong bias among educators to use only heterogeneous groupings. Part of this misunderstanding comes from the prevalence of "tracking," a process by which elementary students were grouped based on test scores, without considering individual needs or maturation. High school students were similarly grouped based on educational goals, such as a "college track" (Clark, 2008). Tracking usually was inflexible, unlike ability grouping. Kulik (1992) emphasized ability grouping is not the same thing, yet these terms frequently are used interchangeably and the inequities of tracking are used to deny ability grouping for gifted learners. Ability grouping in math or reading for advanced instruction, for example, is no more elitist or harmful to the students than grouping the most skilled performers in show choir or athletes on a varsity team and providing them with more challenging learning opportunities. Nevertheless, gifted students frequently are denied similar instruction because it is deemed elitist.

This challenge is not restricted to rural areas, but the more stable, traditional, even insular nature of many rural areas presents fewer opportunities to refute these myths and misunderstandings. Howley, Howley, and Pendarvis (1986) proposed that schools with successful academic programs and stable staff have the best chance of countering these misconceptions. Two points are crucial: Gifted students are at-risk without appropriate education, and programming for them is effective.

Community Perspective

Resistance to Change

Until recently, the smallest communities in rural America have changed little, although the population has become disproportionally older (Colangelo & Davis, 2003). Those who relocate to more urbanized areas in search of jobs, rarely return to their small-town roots. As a result, traditional, conservative values often reign, and there is a tendency to resist change. Rural teachers may have had limited, if any, exposure to the most recent innovative methods of teaching and learning. Although the one-room-schoolhouse mentality may be an advantage in meeting the needs of some gifted learners, teachers still must be trained to identify and address individual student learning levels and abilities. On the other hand, a community's assumptions about educating their children may be as antiquated as chalk and blackboards. No one stands out, differences are largely ignored, and change usually is for the worse.

The economic base of some rural communities is in flux with manufacturing and service industries now moving in. Although the nature of the work may be changing, rural dependence on a single industry is not. Poverty and unemployment are still high, resulting in a limited tax base to fund education (Colangelo & Davis, 2003).

Educational Expectations

In this retro-environment found in some communities, young wives produce offspring to contribute to the agrarian labor force. Attending college in a distant part of the state or country is seldom achieved. Expectations for males and females involve working on the farm, clerking in local stores or gas stations, or repairing machinery. Such limited opportunities can be stifling for gifted youth. In some regions, even finishing high school or attaining a community college education may be uncommon, even in areas that are not particularly isolated.

A no-less-unexpected phenomenon owes its emergence to the rise of telecommuting. Some rural areas have had to contend with new ideas brought in by well-educated professionals relocating from the cities who seek clean air, a less hectic pace, and a safe environment for their children. These individuals' ideas about how to educate their children can clash with those of the native citizens, requiring much discussion and compromise in open forums.

Schools will need to provide career education that includes not only preparing for the more traditional jobs but emphasizing new vocations, skills, communications media, and interactions with others. Both females and males will be exposed to learning options heretofore unimagined, many still in their infancy. Adjusting to this new reality will require a reappraisal of community mores and a willingness to embrace innovation. Gifted youth in particular will need to be exposed to career blending where two or three specialties are merged to suit the individual's interests and talents. Schools will need to provide both academic and career counseling. Lewis and Hafer (2007) recommended citing examples of successful adults who came from rural communities.

Changing Demographics

The demographics in many parts of the country now are beginning to reflect the way the native population is adapting to an influx of immigrants moving to the United States, both legally and illegally, and settling in rural areas. Their cultural influence can quickly envelope the community, most noticeably in the schools. Suddenly there is a need for bilingual teachers who can help students and their parents learn English and find jobs requiring English language fluency.

Additional Challenges

Funding

Educators in rural schools have limited access to many kinds of resources—except for caring people. Although poverty is not as pervasive in rural areas as it once was, it remains a serious concern for many communities.

Funding is the greatest challenge because the tax base frequently is limited (Colangelo et al., 1999; Johnson & Strange, 2007). Too many rural communities struggle with insufficient dollars for competitive teacher salaries and the purchase of educational materials. As a result, students in these schools may not receive an education equal to those in more populous districts with larger tax bases.

Staffing and Teacher Preparation

In these challenging conditions, rural schools often are unable to attract highly qualified teachers with expertise in a range of content areas and training in gifted education. On-site professional development and conference attendance to gain such expertise often is limited by cost and distance. Colangelo et al. (1999) demonstrated that even districts with strong programs often lose them when the educator who supported them leaves. As a result, few programs for gifted students are available in rural areas.

Another challenge exists when there are few gifted learners in a classroom or school. Teachers have little incentive to learn how to adapt methods and materials, so these learners spend most of the class period waiting while the others "catch-up." Teachers may not even notice that some students are capable of more advanced learning, unless they intentionally devise challenging and open-ended instruction.

To further aggravate the issue, educators rarely learn how to work with gifted children during their teacher preparation programs. They frequently are not familiar with the characteristics and needs of gifted students, and the problem is magnified in rural areas because teachers have few opportunities to interact with other educators. In addition, they have access to limited, if any, professional development opportunities related to gifted education. The result is teachers in rural schools may be ill-prepared to recognize and help the precocious students they serve.

All teachers must learn strategies to educate children with advanced educational abilities, not just specialists, for not only the educators who have specialized in the education of the gifted teach gifted learners. This is not just a rural issue but it *is* more challenging in rural schools due to access and incentive.

Benefits and Accommodations

Limited teacher preparation in working with gifted students and a sparse number of intellectual peers are problems. However, in enumerating the challenges facing students in rural schools, some very definite advantages are overshadowed. The National Education Association (NEA; n.d.) lists multi-grade classrooms, peer assistance, mentoring, and cooperative learning as approaches pioneered in rural schools and copied by larger schools. One teacher may combine students from two or more grades in a single elementary class. High schools may establish classes of mixed-aged students as a means of expanding course offerings in the sciences, music and fine arts, foreign language, math, and a range of other specialties.

Some approaches best applied to small classes have been compromised by the trend toward consolidation. Small schools resist because merging forces them to grow bigger and lose their ties to local communities (Colangelo et al., 1999). Colangelo et al. and Montgomery (as cited in Manning & Besnoy, 2008) point out the advantages of "smaller teacher-pupil ratios and community involvement" (p. 126). An obvious benefit of low teacher-student ratios is that each student receives more attention in the classroom, allowing for more individualized instruction. Students also are able to participate in any or all extracurricular activities offered. Students in small schools usually are known by many in the community; consequently they may have exceptional opportunities to learn from others who know and trust them (Colangelo et al., 1999).

Smaller student-to-teacher ratios favor more interaction with teachers. Consequently, these teachers are likely to recognize students' talents and help them advance at the pace they need. Colangelo and Davis (2003) described a high school student who undertook an individualized, in-depth independent study in opera because the school personnel knew him well and trusted him with considerable independence.

Opportunities for Gifted Students in Rural Schools

Despite the rarity of specially designed gifted programs in rural schools, exceptionally talented students have been known to thrive in rural locales. For one thing, these learners are likely to stand out prominently in their small classes if they have good, observant teachers.

A benefit of small schools is fewer decision makers that can offer more latitude in accommodating a gifted student's educational needs. Educators may have to wear multiple hats, but a positive result can be greater curricular flexibility. Most schools with enrollment of less than 100 students get by with one superintendent who doubles as principal and also may teach and coach. The multiple roles may work to the advantage of outstanding students. The factor most likely to influence special academic treatment of these high-ability individuals is an easy informality among the educators about making accommodations for those with high abilities. When only a few students merit content adaptation, teachers of the appropriate subjects spontaneously confer with each other to make the necessary adjustments. The key is high-abilities identification among perceptive educators who know how to provide appropriate instruction.

A student singled out as highly capable in a given discipline can attend a higher grade for instruction in one or more subjects. Providing a form of content acceleration seems to be a natural solution when a student is especially knowledgeable in one or two subjects. Bringing a student to a class with higher level material is more efficient and more coherent than leaving that student to tackle accelerated textbook material on his or her own. In rural schools, grade acceleration is relatively uncomplicated. Parents and teachers have fewer concerns about placing a capable younger student among much older students, because chances are, the families of both are already acquainted (Lewis & Hafer, 2007).

Accommodations for Limited Resources

Educational and community support such as school and community libraries and counseling services are frequently insufficient in rural areas. How can capacity to educate children in such regions, especially gifted children, be increased?

Human Resources

Rural people usually need to be self-sufficient when it comes to running farms, ranches, homes, and communities. Numerous skills and talents can be found in even small communities. People in trades and farmers have developed countless skills that assist in building or mending broken tools and equipment. This practical expertise can involve subject matter useful for gifted learners' education (e.g., chemistry, physics, and engineering). For the creatively minded, some utilitarian skills can be used artistically. Local experts can be tapped to teach a unit on electronics for the physics class, for example. Specialists from universities, the professions, and government can be called upon to share their knowledge with students using conference calls or other technology.

Technology

Digital technologies offer solutions for educators and students alike.

> The intent of electronic technology is not to be an alternative to a high quality teacher and classroom; the intent is to be an alternative to nothing, and that is what many rural gifted students are getting right now. Electronic technology equalizes access to education. (Belcastro, 2002, p. 14)

Belcastro recognized the financial challenge exacerbated by the need for upgraded technology infrastructure and recommends both state and federal governments make broadband access reach into even the most remote communities in our country. All students, in addition to gifted learners, could have access to a high quality of education regardless of local school districts' ability to pay.

Professional development. Much needed professional development can be delivered to educators in remote districts using the same distance technologies or streamed from a central location, such as the state gifted directors' office. Video developed by other state or national specialists and preserved on DVDs can be similarly delivered. The only technology needed to receive the "stream" is a computer with high-speed access to the Internet and the access link. The stream can be captured, stored on a server (if space is available), and posted for asynchronous use. Educators too can avail themselves of additional courses, degrees, and professional development through distance education. For example, gifted certification classes are offered by several universities.

In addition to using technology to provide professional development, some states have "educational service units" of some kind. Districts pay to belong to these consortiums in return for services such as professional development, assessment specialists, financial management, and other supports made possible through pooled dollars. Some small districts band together regionally to form similar consortia whereby specialty teachers instruct students across district lines using technology. Gifted students and others are able to take advanced classes not otherwise available in their own schools (e.g., foreign language, math, science; Clark, 2008). In addition, numerous classes are accessible online permitting rural gifted students educational options found in more populous areas.

Virtual field trips. Opportunities to visit art galleries, foreign lands, great buildings, libraries, museums, national parks, science demonstrations, and theaters are as near as the click of a computer mouse given an Internet connection. Electronic tours and demonstrations expose isolated rural students to experiences enjoyed by more affluent and centrally located students. An Internet connection can bring the vast resources of the world to every corner of the globe.

Social networks. Blogs, listservs, e-mail, and Voice Over IP are electronic communication systems for enabling interaction and socialization between gifted students that can lessen the extreme sense of isolation they experience. These technologies have potential for enriching students' academics and building social structures among individuals with similar interests, and satisfying, at least in part, emotional needs. Adults must monitor children and youth, not allowing then to roam the Internet unsupervised any more than in the physical world.

Counseling. Counseling services frequently are unavailable in rural communities. Cooperative arrangements need to be made with other school districts that do have qualified counselors. Online counseling using synchronous virtual chats and asynchronous discussion board meetings are two options for building the necessary affective support in lieu of face-to-face sessions (Lewis & Hafer, 2007). Counseling using one of several Web-based options (e.g., NetMeeting, polycom, Skype Web conferencing) now available offer alternate approaches with

> real-time audio/visual communication that can help fill the gap for personal or group counseling. Transmission is point to point from the transmitter to the receiver so

the counselor would be able to control who had access, thus providing a reasonable measure of confidentiality. (Lewis & Hafer, 2007, Educational resources may be unavailable, para. 2)

Research. Local and school library books and services can be expanded by working with a college librarian to enable the loan of books and access to other resources, such as digital copies of journal articles, electronic databases, and tutorials for distance access to library tools. Many books are downloadable from the online Project Gutenberg (see http://www.gutenberg.us).

Another challenge in teaching the gifted in rural settings is that most program models are designed for use in suburban and urban settings. Numerous instructional paradigms are available as a framework when developing or revising a program of services for gifted students (e.g., Clark, 2008; Davis & Rimm, 2004; Karnes & Stephens, 2008; Reis & Renzulli, 1982; VanTassel-Baska & Stambaugh, 2006). Each has merit but will not be suitable for all school districts. Indeed, using carefully selected components from several models allows services to be tailored to meet local needs.

Program Development

With the rapid increase in new branches of knowledge in the last few decades, it is all the more important that "programs for gifted students . . . address substantive academic goals, whatever their instructional or curricular design" (Luhman & Fundis, 1989, Academic outcomes, para. 1). Luhman and Fundis recommended rural educators ask questions during program development so local characteristics are accommodated. Such questions might include:

- What academic (and affective) outcomes are desired?
- What services are effective for achieving those outcomes?
- Given the available resources, how can the services be implemented?
- Given the necessity of local support, how can student performance be evaluated best so as to achieve transparency for would-be supporters?

Best practice would be to offer rural students a comprehensive program that meets their need for rigorous and relevant academic learning. Such a program would employ acceleration and quality enrichment; process skill development; flexible grouping; and academic, career, and affective counseling. Although a full spectrum of services is desirable, rural educators are advised to first choose only those services that meet students' most immediate needs, then strive to develop the rest while the initial components are being implemented. It is far better to start small than do nothing at all.

Borland (1989) described a systematic approach to developing a gifted program. Authorities in the field (e.g., Borland, 1989; Clark, 2008; Davis & Rimm, 2004; Delisle & Lewis, 2003; VanTassel-Baska, 2003a) tend to agree on the major components. First, the district's teachers and administrators must arrive at a workable definition of giftedness. They may choose to use the state's definition, the federal definition, or a modified version specific to the district's capacity for providing services. Next, a planning committee with enthusiastic representatives from each major stakeholder group (parents, teachers, administrators, community members, etc.) needs to be assembled (Clark, 2008). This committee will work to establish the district's philosophy of gifted education, program goals, identification procedures, specialized instruction, and plan for program evaluation. Each element must complement the others so that the program is coordinated and coherent. Furthermore, district planning needs to envision a continuum of services to meet the diverse needs of gifted students in pre-K through grade 12 (National Association for Gifted Children [NAGC], 1998). Lewis, Cruzeiro, and Hall (2007) advocated for evaluating the gifted program's goals as part of the schoolwide improvement plan. Such data then can be disaggregated along with other school assessment data. With data teams working to improve the learning of *all* students, the gifted program will be better integrated with general education.

Rural "program planners must remember that a local program is intended to meet local needs to the extent allowed by local resources" (Clark, 2008, p. 489), and they should be sized accordingly. In addition, gifted programs can positively influence the quality of the entire curriculum and expand career opportunities while encouraging greater academic success for students. As a result, teachers and staff will be more committed to sustaining what has been created from their collective labors (Pitts, 1986, as cited in Clark, 2008). The planners, teachers, and staff may have to improvise and exert considerable effort during the development stage, but the successful program they create, even in small and isolated schools, will produce a legacy of thriving gifted learners.

Regardless of size or proximity to a large population center, rural school districts should follow some basic guidelines when developing their own gifted programs. NAGC (1998) made several recommendations that can be applied to rural gifted education programs:

- Students should be pretested on basic knowledge and skill proficiency and mastered material should be replaced with more challenging content and instruction.
- "Teachers must differentiate, replace, supplement, or modify curricula to facilitate higher level learning goals" (p. 8).
- Gifted underachievers should not be denied more demanding instruction. It may be the challenge that will motivate the child to achieve. Lay mentors sometimes can be recruited to help motivate individuals.

- "Gifted learners who are at risk must have special attention, counseling, and support to help them realize their full potential" (p. 4). Any counselor working with gifted individuals should be familiar with their unique needs. This important requirement is made much more difficult in rural areas because certified personnel are frequently unavailable. The principal (or counselor if one is available) should keep a current list of regional resource centers that may offer emotional counseling.
- All teachers working with gifted learners need to understand their characteristics, including social and emotional traits, as well as how to educate them appropriately. In rural schools, this might mean providing professional development for all educators by means of off-site resources such as video conferencing, distance learning via the Internet, and commercially produced tutorials.

Identification

Among gifted learners there are children with singular needs that many teachers and parents haven't encountered. Identifying and serving this population is always challenging because their characteristics are so diverse. Children culturally or linguistically different, those twice-exceptional, and the disadvantaged from low-income homes often are difficult to identify and serve. Once recognized, they need instruction adapted to their unique blend of strengths and deficits.

The most common methods for identifying giftedness in school are intelligence tests, achievement tests, domain-specific aptitude tests, student grades, and teacher recommendations. Increasingly, nontraditional assessments also are being developed to identify students frequently missed by conventional methods (VanTassel-Baska, 2003a). The latter include nonverbal ability tests, creativity tests, student portfolios, and performance by audition. Still, others have relied on performance-based assessment and parent, peer, and community recommendations. Johnsen

(2004) strongly recommends combining quantitative measures (tests) with qualitative assessment (portfolios, performance, recommendations) so students' best performances can be observed and used in the decision-making process.

Developing defensible identification procedures is not easy, although the reduced bureaucracy often found in rural districts can expedite procedures. Giftedness can be viewed as absolute or relative, depending on school policy. Identifying students who perform at a high level relative to their peers and their own background has become more common (VanTassel-Baska, 2003a) as well as practical for rural educators. Their first question becomes: Which students are performing above their grade level in one or more content areas? The second is: What assessment methods besides tests identify these students? Methods selected need to consider the range of individual differences and be convincingly explainable. VanTassel-Baska (2003a) stated that the task is to include students who would benefit from enhanced educational opportunities at any given time rather than only identifying "truly gifted" students. Students from underserved populations, among others, would have more opportunities to receive services designed to enhance their skills and confidence, thus affording them the opportunity for additional advanced instruction. With this model, students would be reassessed regularly to determine if their placement is right for them.

Multidimensional assessment is the key to defensible assessment. NAGC (1998) standards stated "no single assessment instrument or its results [should deny] student eligibility for gifted programming services" (p. 2). Both Johnsen (2004) and VanTassel-Baska (2003a) stressed the value of screening and identification phases, rather than the more common group achievement and intelligence test approach that relies on a very high qualifying score (e.g., 98th percentile). Johnsen addresses decision-making as a separate phase, based on the data gathered in the two earlier phases.

The screening phase should give every student in the school the opportunity to be considered (Johnsen, 2004; NAGC, 1998).

Multiple assessments should consist of both tests and nontest methods in order to be comprehensive. Both performance-based assessment and dynamic assessment in students' areas of strength are approaches that may help find students whose talents might not otherwise be discovered. Dynamic assessment determines how quickly a student can learn new, challenging information when given the opportunity,

The second phase, identification, uses more refined assessment methods, including individually administered tests to gain a better measure of student needs. Van Tassel-Baska (2003b) suggested using "off-level aptitude and achievement measures—such as the PLUS test, the School, College, and Ability Test (SCAT), and the SAT—to ascertain a true dispersion of the student's scores in order to select the most able" (p. 89). Johnsen (2004) advocated employing a case study, profile, or minimum score approach for defensible selection. Each model uses all data gathered in both phases—screening and identification. To be included in the district's gifted program, students must meet the score criteria minus the standard error of measurement for some but not all of the scores. Johnsen recommended requiring at least one quantitative and one qualitative score for eligibility and explains procedures for calculating the standard error of measurement for non-test assessments. This method has the benefit of giving more opportunity to students from underserved populations.

Educators in rural districts may decide that screening alone will find those few students in their small schools who need advanced instruction. They need to use one of Johnsen's (2004) recommended selection methods; accountability is important regardless of the size of the district. Finally, rural educators need to tailor their identification methods to the services they are able to provide. Recording numbers of gifted students just for its own sake cannot be justified.

These are the commonly recommended methods for the identification ↔ placement model of gifted education. On the other hand, Birch (2004) described an "assess ↔ educate" model for evaluating and prescribing instruction that would be easier to implement in smaller schools than in larger ones and would benefit all children in addition to those who are gifted.

> When individualized, adaptive models of instruction are the mode, gifted children, and all other children, receive the kind of education that optimizes their opportunities. By definition, adaptive education matches the content, the pace, and the teaching style of education to each child's interests, abilities, and potentials. (Birch, 2004, p. 7)

Birch explained that "individualized" education does not necessarily mean teachers work with each child separately. Rather, they employ flexible grouping strategies to facilitate instructing students at similar levels, depending on content and student need. Instruction and assessment are interdependent, one leading to the other in a progression toward optimal learning for all.

Identifying challenging instructional needs for any student must occur regardless of the selected model. Once students are recognized as needing more challenging learning opportunities, instruction can be adapted using a wide range of options.

Instruction

Maker and Nielson (1996), among many other gifted specialists (e.g., Roberts & Inman, 2007; Robinson, Shore, & Enersen, 2007; VanTassel-Baska, 2003b), emphasized adapting a school's curriculum based on the characteristics of the gifted learners served. They endorse specific strategies based on the following learning behaviors:

- humor,
- motivation,
- interests,
- inquiry,
- problem solving,
- sensitivity,

- intuition,
- reasoning,
- imagination/creativity,
- memory/knowledge/understanding, and
- learning. (Maker & Nielson, 1996, pp. 25–27)

Regardless of whether a student displays many of these behaviors or only a few, teachers should modify their instruction accordingly, even without formal identification.

"How?" is the big question. Teachers of small classes have the advantage of becoming more intimately acquainted with their students' strengths and weaknesses, as do teachers in small communities who know their students even before they come to school. Being aware of those student learning behaviors that require differentiation (for strengths and weaknesses) is the first step.

Differentiation involves four main aspects of the curriculum: content, process, product, and environment (Maker & Nielson, 1996). The following instructional techniques are universally applicable and readily adaptable to rural-school needs.

Content Modifications

In order to adapt content based on students' readiness, teachers must have acquired competence in their subject area(s) that applies not only to the level they teach but also to the content that precedes and follows it. They need curricular depth to provide not only basic facts, but also conceptual knowledge and generalizations to help students develop connections between important concepts. Maker and Nielson (1996) stated:

> Gifted learners need to spend much less time on concrete information and little time in drill and practice in their area or areas of giftedness. The development of abstract concepts, derivation of generalizations, and induction of unknown principals is a much more effective use of their learning time. (p. 75)

Teachers in small, as well as large, schools can modify the content for gifted students by allowing them to investigate the current class topic in greater depth (enrichment) instead of spending most of their time learning basic facts. Content selection for all students should consider whether the topic is worth students' time, considering the rapid pace that knowledge is accumulating. The content needs to be "conceptually complex to render it meaningful for gifted students" and the teacher needs to be capable of imparting it effectively (VanTassel-Baska & Stambaugh, 2006, p. 20).

Numerous specialists (e.g., Clark, 2008; Maker & Nielson, 1996; VanTassel-Baska, 2003a) recommended the use of broad-based concepts to provide structure for the many facts students assimilate and to connect these big ideas to life lessons. Change, discovery, patterns, relationships, and systems are but a few examples. Avery and Little (2003, p. 107) described the process of implementing the concept *change* with the following generalizations that apply to any content area:

- Change is everywhere.
- Change is linked to time.
- Change may be positive or negative.
- Change may happen naturally or be caused by people.
- Change may be perceived as orderly or random.

Little (2003) provided a sample lesson implementing the change concept in a study of poetry that effectively demonstrates the substantive and engaging learning possible for gifted learners (see p. 136 of that work). For teachers who would prefer ready-made yet high quality instruction, VanTassel-Baska and her colleagues at The College of William and Mary have developed concept-based units for language arts, science, and social studies published by Kendall-Hunt and Prufrock Press.

The process of "compacting," eliminating repetitive instruction and practicing already mastered content, is a structured method of offering advanced material while still being accountable to school, parents, and community (Reis et al., 1993). Math is an easy subject to compact because of its essentially hierarchical structure; however, the same process applies to all subjects at all school levels. For example, if Kaylie already knows basic addition and subtraction facts in kindergarten or first grade, she needs to move on to larger numbers and their practical application. As she demonstrates readiness, she can concentrate on the next operations: multiplication and division.

Teachers informally determine students' readiness for advanced skills through visiting and observing students and counseling with parents. Formally, they confirm their observations through the process of pretesting such as end-of-unit worksheets or quizzes and above-grade-level testing. The teacher might observe Kaylie counting by two's, five's, or the like; grouping blocks and adding them; or looking at a plate of cookies and stating there aren't enough for each child to each have two. Observation can demonstrate when Kaylie is ready to move on to more challenging learning.

Advanced, in-depth content can be delivered to the student in elementary school until the teacher's skill level is exceeded. Then the student needs to move on to instruction at a higher level using technology (e.g., CDs, Web-based courses) or a mentor needs to be located from the middle or high school (teacher or student), the community, or through a community college or university to provide the content support. Fortunately for students in rural areas, the technology for transmitting instruction across vast distances seems to increase daily.

Process Modifications

Content isn't the only area to be modified for gifted learners. The processes by which teachers impart learning and the way students work to process what they are learning are just as important. A multitude of methods can be used to adapt the process of instruction and learning for gifted children.

Choosing alternatives. All students benefit from having some real choice in content, process, and product. Letting them assume responsibility for their own learning ensures the classroom will be truly learner-centered. Maker and Nielson (1996) emphasized student freedom of choice in several respects: "topics to study, methods to use in the process . . . the type of products to create, and the context of the learning environment" (p. 120). Where else would students, teachers, and parents cooperate so readily in a joint venture to let students take the lead in deciding what and how to learn?

Colangelo et al. (1999) shared an anecdote from a high school senior who valued the opportunity he was given to conduct an extensive independent study of opera because the principal knew and trusted him. Teachers of any age student can begin as they would with very young children—by providing a limited selection of choices either in the area of content, process, or product. Maker and Nielson (1996) cautioned not to allow more freedom than the student can learn from and manage and that the teacher can accept, because it requires yielding some control.

Contracts and agendas. There are several management strategies teachers can use to give gifted learners structure as they work more independently than other children in the classroom. Winebrenner (2001) shared several kinds of contracts along with behavioral expectations particularly suited to elementary students; however, the basic ideas could easily be adapted for secondary level.

The "personal agenda" (Tomlinson, 1999) is more of a guide to the tasks the independent learner will be responsible for during a stated period of time. Special instructions can be included for each task as reminders of teacher expectations; for instance, remember to use good grammar or use resources beyond encyclopedias. Students can complete the agenda items in any order unless otherwise directed. This strategy, primarily for elementary students, would work very well for secondary students and could be used in conjunction with a contract if desired. Tomlinson describes how all students could work on their agendas at certain times of the day allowing the whole class a measure of freedom. In addition, the agendas would be personalized for students' readiness. Those needing extra practice or less challenging exercises would not be conspicuous. The teacher would be free to monitor individual students or introduce new skills to small groups.

Curriculum compacting. A strategy Renzulli and Smith defined in 1978, curriculum compacting differs from *acceleration* in that students' content mastery is assessed and replacement activities are prescribed based on assessment results (as cited in Robinson et al., 2007; Rogers, 2002). According to these researchers, up to half the general curriculum can be replaced for high-ability elementary students without affecting test scores in "reading, mathematics concepts, and social studies, even when testing is a grade level above standard class placement" (Robinson et al., 2007, p. 117). Rogers (2002) asserted this apparent anomaly stems from adopting a curriculum with low expectations devoid of the challenge gifted children need, leaving them stuck "repeating information they already know" (p. 116).

To reconfigure the standard curriculum for a gifted learner, the teacher needs to set an acceptable level of mastery, say 85%, before pretesting. The assessment may be the end-of-unit test, a teacher-made test of key concepts, or one of several informal assessments such as reviewing the student's past work in the subject being considered for compacting. Rogers (2002) described additional assessment methods and provided a chart profiling children who would be good candidates for compacting. Once mastered, content is replaced by high-quality extension activities to move the student through the content. Preparing appropriate replacement activities in advance will ease this transition. Teachers need continuous professional development and peer support to be successful in implementing compacting for students (Robinson et al., 2007).

Although compacting is most common at the elementary level, it can be used in middle and high schools too. Its advantage for all teachers is that it offers justification for assigning some students alternative lessons. Educators could thus defend educational decisions to all stakeholders, something especially important to small communities.

Differentiated assessments. If instruction is presented at different levels of sophistication, assessments should be treated similarly. Roberts and Inman (2007) have devised what they term the Developing and Assessing Products Tool (DAP Tool). Components in this modular approach to rubrics include *content, presentation, creativity,* and *reflection* at three challenge levels, each with the same six-point rating scale. In their book, rubrics for five common products are provided at each level, facilitating transition to this authentic assessment method. One of several advantages of the DAP Tool is that rubrics "don't limit students' learning by setting the learning ceiling at proficiency" (Roberts & Inman, 2007, p. 142).

Evidence of reasoning. Requiring evidence of reasoning is a metacognitive skill that continues to benefit gifted students long after a specific lesson. It is essential that gifted learners be able to explain not only how they formulate a solution to a problem in any subject but also that they furnish logical evidence to support their solutions. Maker and Nielson (1996) discussed the empowering benefits of requiring gifted students to provide evidence to support their reasoning. One effective method to elicit such reasoning is the Socratic method—posing questions whose answers expose strong or weak reasoning. Such open-ended discussions often give rise to deliberation that may challenge conventional belief systems. This is a risk teachers need to be willing to take while probing for valid supporting evidence.

Habits of mind. Students learn to think like and apply attitudes, predispositions, and skills of professionals in a given field (VanTassel-Baska & Stambaugh, 2006). This method of thinking could be presented to all students to a certain extent and expanded for gifted learners.

High-level thinking skills. Gifted learners need higher level thinking skills—analysis, synthesis, evaluation—rather than conventional knowledge and comprehension levels. "Critical thinking, creative thinking, creative problem solving, and real-world skills such as decision making, planning, and forecasting" attract the attention of these advanced thinkers (Maker &

Nielson, 1996, p. 97). Metacognition is "reflection on one's learning processes . . . [including] planning, monitoring, and assessing [one's] own learning for efficient and effective use of time and resources" (VanTassel-Baska & Stambaugh, 2006, p. 13). Like other high-level processing, it should not be reserved solely for gifted students; however, they need more opportunity to engage in such thought processes.

Independent study. Students can work independently of the regular class assignments in some or all subjects. The student, regardless of age, still needs the teacher's guidance, attention, and caring. Few students will work alone for long periods of time without the instructor checking progress and answering questions, although some gifted students require privacy. Part of a teacher's job for all students is to demonstrate nurturing pedagogy.

Inquiry. This strategy involves questioning and metacognition. It is promoted in classroom environments in which students are responsible for their own learning, deciding what information is needed, where to find it, and how to make use of what they learn (e.g., problem-based learning; VanTassel-Baska & Stambaugh, 2006). Depending on the classroom dynamics, inquiry might be more effective with cluster-grouped or cross-age-grouped gifted students.

Menu boards. A strategy used by several gifted specialists to accommodate student readiness and interest is the menu board (see Roberts & Inman, 2007; Tomlinson, 1999; Winebrenner, 2001). Kindergarteners might have only four activities while older students could have 9, 12, 16, 25, or more depending on the intended learning. Tomlinson and Winebrenner offered the option for students to propose a few of their own ideas in place of those provided by the teacher. They are approved for that child by the teacher. Activities can be completed in any sequence, and can be generic (usable for any content or purpose) or unit specific.

Tomlinson (1999) described using two menu boards with different task levels, one at grade level (see Figure 1) and the other at a challenge level (see Figure 2). These boards are used as part of the instruction for all students. Within the space provided,

❑ Using the book, *The Girl in Blue*, write a newspaper editorial on the war from the point of view of one character.	❑ Answer the following: How did the Confederate Navy help in the war?	❑ Write a letter home from the battle. Include enough details so that the setting is apparent.

Figure 1. Partial example of a Civil War menu board for typical students.

Note. Reproduced with permission from Stacey Gibb.

○ Using the book, *The Girl in Blue*, compare the account in the book to what you know based on the battle you have chosen (and researched).	○ Compare/contrast how the blockade and the abolitionist movement affected the war, and how it affected the battle chosen, in particular.	○ Write a letter home from the battle. Describe the living conditions and the morale of the soldiers. Include enough details so that the setting is apparent.

Figure 2. Partial example of a Civil War menu board for gifted students.

Note. Reproduced with permission from Stacey Gibb.

which may be a square for one group and a circle for another, students check off each cell as it is completed in any order. She wrote that students don't seem to notice the different levels of difficulty because the basic tasks are similar and interesting.

Roberts and Inman (2007) presented examples of menus as optional learning experiences for students who pretest out of a unit, as a project to accompany a unit based on student interest, as a motivational semester review, and as a unit assessment of content not tied to conventional ways of demonstrating knowledge. The authors described how to adapt the menu for learning style or modality, multiple intelligences, student interest, and readiness or ability level, and how to implement the menus in the classroom.

Open-ended instruction. Open-ended instruction is essential. It erases the ceiling for students' learning and can be observed in their products. It "implies a difference in teacher attitude reflected in (a) questioning techniques and content of questions,

(b) the design of learning activities and materials, and (c) evaluating of students' responses to questions" (Maker & Nielson, 1996, p. 105). A little extra lesson planning can pay dividends in determining which students will receive questions requiring them to respond in more challenging ways—striving for divergent rather than convergent responses.

Teachers need to be willing to relinquish leadership of the class to honor student expertise that may exceed their own. They will need to be confident enough to permit more student control over what is learned and how. Once teachers open up approaches to learning, they face evaluating those responses and products. Assessment with well-conceived rubrics can ease the challenge. Roberts and Inman (2007) described differentiated grading rubrics in a step-by-step manner that will make this frequently difficult skill easier for any teacher.

Pace. Perhaps the most important process modification teachers can employ to enhance the learning of gifted students is pace, the speed at which new material is imparted (Maker & Nielson, 1996). Gifted students need few repetitions to achieve mastery in their areas of strength. Maker and Nielson and other specialists (e.g., Clark, 2008; VanTassel-Baska, 1998) recommended interdisciplinary instruction based on broad conceptual themes (e.g., change, discovery, systems) to increase the learning value for gifted students who can quickly make complex connections, yet the strategy can be used in heterogeneous classes to increase learning for all students.

Another pacing suggestion Winebrenner (2001) called "hardest first" entails encouraging gifted learners to select several of the hardest problems first. In math, for example, they might attempt to complete the last five problems on the page or in the unit. If they can do so correctly without help, they have proved they understand the skills and can move on to another activity both they and their teacher agree on. Winebrenner emphasized that one error be permitted in order to avoid reinforcing possible perfectionist tendencies. A careless mistake is not an indication of poor understanding. The same principle can be used for application, analysis, or evaluation types of questions at the end of a chapter or unit in other subjects such as science. Rather than answering low-level questions on different kinds of biomes, gifted students could demonstrate mastery of content by applying their knowledge to analyzing the components of a particular biome or comparing two different biomes.

Preassessment. Regardless of the strategy chosen for differentiation, the level of assignment for each student needs to be determined by preassessment. How else will a teacher know if the planned instruction will build on what all children in the class have already learned in content and skills? Roberts and Inman (2007) described a variety of methods for preassessing including, but not limited to, "end-of-the-previous-unit assessment, end-of-the-unit assessment, K-W-L, mind map, the five most difficult questions, open-ended question, interest and experience inventory, and the adapted Situational Leadership model" (p. 38). Although teachers remain dubious, the time spent pretesting and documenting results will save time, as Reis et al. (1993) documented in their extensive curriculum compacting study.

Tiered instructional strategies. Teachers need to employ tiered assignments to provide instruction at optimal learning levels and entry points for the range of student abilities and readiness found in most classrooms, not just for gifted students. Offering only the same level of instruction for all learners is not an effective strategy. Tomlinson (1999) exposed the fallacy behind "teaching to the middle":

> A student who struggles with reading or has a difficult time with abstract thinking nonetheless needs to make sense of pivotal concepts and principles in a given chapter or story. Simultaneously, a student who is advanced well beyond grade expectations in the same subject needs to find genuine challenge in working with the same concepts and principles. (p. 83)

Tomlinson (1999) stressed that all students need to be taught key skills using "respectful" activities for everyone. In tiered lessons, the content remains the same but the approaches used to teach and learn it differ. All students begin learning where they are and the progress they make ensures they feel successful. The use of her Equalizer model helps establish a hierarchy of degrees of "abstractness, complexity, and open-endedness" (Tomlinson, 1999, p. 83). Refer to Tomlinson (1999) for an explanation of the methods for creating tiered lessons.

Product Modifications

The way students demonstrate their learning, the product, can be differentiated with little difficulty in any school. It is an open-ended opportunity for encouraging gifted students to extend their learning. Karnes and Stephens (2000) compiled a thorough resource featuring 101 kinds of products and how to use them. Students have the opportunity to engage their creativity to further enhance their learning. A fifth grader, Becca, thought oral reports were boring. So, when it was her turn to present her report on a state, she dressed like a professional, set out a map of New York, and borrowed the teacher's pointer. In the manner of a tour guide, she extolled the virtues of the Empire State. She had fun and so did the class. This example illustrates an oral product. Students should be encouraged to tackle other types of products (e.g., visual, written, kinesthetic) to develop proficiency in areas that might not be strengths but are skills they will need as adults.

Gifted education specialists recommend that product expectations for gifted learners be similar to those expected for professionals. Maker and Nielson (1996) listed criteria teachers need to consider when differentiating products for gifted learners: The focus should be on a real problem for a real purpose and a real audience, and evaluated by people in the field using criteria from their field—rather than a contrived assignment to demonstrate certain skills evaluated only by the teacher. The product should synthesize or transform the information rather than paraphrase material from sources. Format should be appropriate for the product and selected by the student. Gifted students gain far more academically by being expected to produce at such a high level. Teachers in rural schools can differentiate the product component of learning as well as suburban or urban teachers, particularly given the extensive resources of the Internet.

Environment Modifications

Reconfiguring the environment is indispensable when modifying content, process, or product for gifted learners. Maker and Nielson (1996) described the connections between gifted students' characteristics and modifying the environment to more appropriately enhance their learning. These strategies are readily adaptable to rural schools regardless of size.

Acceptance versus judgment. This principle "is characterized more by the avoidance of value judgments than by the absence of restrictions and the encouragement of divergence" (Maker & Nielson, 1996, p. 46). Teachers can accept a child while not condoning an inappropriate behavior or agreeing with a controversial opinion. It is difficult for any child to grow in a judgmental atmosphere.

Complexity versus simplicity. Gifted students usually appreciate environments rich in options for learning—from the spatial arrangement of the classroom to the displays on the walls and bulletin boards. Even a small room reserved for gifted students of all ages can provide them a sense of ownership and creativity. They can gather, arrange different kinds of relaxation and study options, and decorate the room for more varied visual stimulation. Maker and Nielson (1996) recommended including displays that demonstrate links between disciplines and relationships between concepts and processes.

Flexibility versus rigidity. Furniture can be rearranged to accommodate different educational settings, such as learning centers, small groups, demonstrations, and performances. This allows for learning to take place in a variety of informal placements rather than in rigid rows of desks or at large tables. Learning should not be confined to a classroom or to certain times of day. Teachers may achieve better results introducing reading or physics under a tree outside on a beautiful day than in a stuffy classroom. They can alter an elementary school day at times to accommodate a special need or opportunity. In small schools, high school teachers may be free to vary class length so a gifted student could complete assignments more quickly. Gifted students thrive when teachers relax arbitrary "time constraints," allowing for greater depth of study in areas of particular interest (Maker & Nielson, 1996, p. 61). "Flexibility, in essence, is demonstrated by a willingness to change—either room arrangements or routines—so that students will feel they are an integral part of an effective, functional, learning community" (Maker & Nielson, 1996, p. 63).

Independence versus dependence. Maker and Nielson (1996) emphasized the interconnections between learner-centered classrooms and the process skills of open-ended instruction and student choice. Together they hasten gifted students becoming independent learners. A vital goal for educators of gifted students is to help them maximize their skills and talents by becoming autonomous learners. Gifted students usually thrive on less formal learning than nongifted students who could be given some responsibility for their own learning with progress monitored using contracts.

High mobility versus low mobility. The discretionary freedom to learn that a student enjoys inside or outside the classroom is related to the independence and flexibility continuums. According to Maker and Nielson (1996), gifted students need to be free to direct their own activities and assume responsibility for what and how they learn. Off-site rural settings may even be necessary and more accessible for gifted youth with special interests. A dairy, fishery, pond, and a plot of land for a student garden offer rich learning experiences in conjunction with community mentors.

Learner-centered versus teacher-centered. The former encourages the formation of a learning community where the teacher's job is to determine what the students have learned previously and design learning opportunities that satisfy school requirements and student interests. Teachers do not serve as the sole determiners and transmitters of content as in the teacher-centered classroom. When the teacher is no longer the principal lesson planner and class director, students begin to take the initiative in acquiring knowledge for themselves (Maker & Nielson, 1996). Although not easy for educators, parents, or students to embrace, the learner-centered environment may prove easier to implement in small schools and communities where families know and trust a particular teacher's judgment.

Open versus closed. The intent is not only to be open to individual differences but to encourage gifted students to avoid uniformity and for students and their families to endorse teaching styles that promote original learning.

Varied groupings versus similar groupings. This modification for gifted learners is one of the easiest for teachers to enact regardless of class size or school location. Within-class groupings need to differ depending on several factors, including the nature of the task, both academically and socially. More options are available than just heterogeneity or grouping by gender, such as interest, learning style, readiness, and ability. Research has focused primarily on upper elementary and middle school students, but many of the grouping options can be used K–12. Students may be grouped across classes at the same or different grades, allowing students of all achievement levels to receive targeted instruction that more closely meets their readiness needs. The number of group members can be varied too, permitting students to gain experience working with large and small groups, pairs, or alone.

Mentoring

Gifted children are just that—children. They need teachers to help them discover and enhance their strengths and compensate for any cognitive and affective challenges. Mentors offer one-on-one socialization in addition to exceptional talent development. Clasen and Clasen (2003) cited studies indicating multiple mentors with different skills and experiences are beneficial for many gifted learners and are especially important for the highly gifted. Older students might be able to mentor younger students, and community members can share relevant skills.

Mentor selection is an important consideration for a successful experience for both parties. In some rural communities this can present an insurmountable challenge unless telementoring is explored. Close personal contact, usually a hallmark of the mentoring relationship, is more difficult to achieve across vast distances. Nevertheless, with the rapidly expanding free technological options using the Internet, including audio/video conferences, many of the drawbacks of distance relationships are reduced. A gifted child living on a large cattle ranch on the vast plains of Montana or in a remote valley in West Virginia can work with a teacher in another district, a specialist from business or profession, or a university professor. The ability to carefully screen and match potential mentors with mentees is reduced, but not entirely absent. Some online sites do a great deal of that work with telementoring (see the Resources section of this book).

Distance Education

Options for transmitting instruction from one location to one or more distant sites using various technologies have increased dramatically over the last 10 to 15 years. Although Colangelo et al. (1999) recognized the increasing role of technology, they stress it "cannot serve as a substitute for peer interaction and collective work" (p. 29). Nevertheless, real-time audio–video communication methods now facilitate quality instruction and even group work to be conducted between distant sites using free Internet-based software (e.g., http://www.skype.com, which requires a computer with a camera), NetMeeting, Internet Protocol (see http://www.polycom.com, uses a polycom). Additional options are available for a fee that cash-strapped districts might negotiate with the venders.

A wide range of classes not offered locally are available to students online. If gifted students are equipped with computers and Internet access, they can be connected for cooperative work with intellectual peers, even in remote areas. Wikis could be used for collaborative assignments allowing cross-site groupings. Although working in the same room is preferable, these new methods can go a long way to ameliorating the dearth of social and emotional supports in addition to connecting isolated gifted learners with trained teachers and the requisite skills for students' future success.

Conclusion

The adage that it takes a village to raise a child applies aptly to educating some gifted children. Close-knit rural communities can be welcoming places to youth with special abilities. Public schools are ill-prepared, in many cases, to serve children outside the typical population. However, flexible, caring, rural educators can be encouraged to craft their instruction to instill in all students the level of learning each requires.

Rural schools, while facing many challenges, are uniquely positioned to adapt what and how they teach to accommodate individual capabilities. The small student body allows every child to stand out and draw the attention of knowledgeable educators.

This volume began with a focus on the challenges confronting schools in rural locations and how to surmount them. The central theme has been to encourage and assist educators who see a need for offering accelerated and more challenging instruction to those with special gifts of intelligence, insight, keen observation, creativity, and a consuming desire to expand their understanding of the world—rural and beyond. These young persons are a precious repository of the insights, experiences, and aspirations gleaned from former generations. Their immeasurable, future contributions to our ever-changing world should be encouraged.

Online Courses

Johns Hopkins University's Center for Talented Youth (CTY)
http://www.cty.jhu.edu/ts/index.html
A talent search program that provides an extensive list of individually paced online courses and other resources.

Class.com
http://www.class.com
This company, originally developed through a grant from the University of Nebraska–Lincoln, offers quality online classes for educators, parents, and students who need additional or different educational options.

Duke University's Talent Identification Program (Duke TIP)
http://www.tip.duke.edu

This site features a talent search program with multiple support services in addition to e-Studies and Independent Learning, including an online newsletter for parents.

Stanford University's Education Program for Gifted Youth (EPGY)
http://epgy.stanford.edu
This program has a long history of serving gifted students with distance courses. An online high school also is available.

Hoagie's (Free) Online High School Courses & Curriculum Materials
http://www.hoagiesgifted.org/online_hs.htm
This site contains links to extensive course collections by content area.

University of Nebraska—Lincoln Independent Study High School
http://highschool.unl.edu
Young gifted students can take classes with students from many locations. This school serves rural and military families.

E-Tours

The British Museum
http://www.britishmuseum.org/explore/online_tours.aspx

Louvre Museum
http://www.louvre.fr/liv/commun/home.jsp?bmLocale=en

National Gallery of Art
http://www.nga.gov/onlinetours/index.shtm

Virtual Tour of Shakespeare's Globe Theatre
http://www.shakespeares-globe.org/virtualtour

Virtual Tours
http://www.virtualfreesites.com/tours.html

Yellowstone National Park
http://www.yellowstone.net/onlinetours

Online Instructional Support Materials

Ask-a-Geologist
http://walrus.wr.usgs.gov/docs/ask-a-ge.html
Questions are answered in 24 hours that aren't already sup-plied through their FAQs. This is one feature of the larger U.S. Geological Society science site that shares science for a changing world. Maps and aerial photographs and satellite images are only a few support materials available from the parent site.

Ask a Mad Scientist
http://www.madsci.org/submit.html
This question-and-answer site is only one small part of the Mad Scientist Network. Lab experiments, archives of information and resources are only two or the many options available for science lovers.

College Countdown
http://www.collegecountdownkit.com
This site shares information to help students prepare for college. A book also is available.

Library of Congress
http://www.loc.gov
The library makes original documents and other resources avail-able online.

MacTutor History of Mathematics Archive
http://turnbull.mcs.st-and.ac.uk/~history

This archive contains far-reaching materials for the math enthusiast and researcher.

Thinkfinity
http://www.thinkfinity.org
The site makes a broad selection of free resources available and is supported by a long list of national content partners.

National Geographic
http://www.nationalgeographic.com
The photos and stories that have made the magazine a treasured resource are available online. One link has activities, games, stories, and videos in addition to animals, people, and places that are of special interest to children.

Project Gutenberg
http://www.gutenberg.org/wiki/Main_Page
This searchable site indexes past and current literature particularly in English, but also in numerous other languages.

ThinkQuest Library
http://www.thinkquest.org/library
ThinkQuest is a competition. The site contains more than 7,000 Web sites created by students around the world who competed in ThinkQuest.

Write to Dr. Math
http://www.mathforum.org/dr.math/ask
The parent site, The Math Forum @ Drexel, contains math supports from simple calculations to complex math.

Gifted Education Support

A Nation Deceived: How Schools Hold Back America's Brightest Students
http://www.accelerationinstitute.org/Nation_Deceived

Obtain a copy of this two-volume set on the effectiveness of acceleration as an option for gifted learners.

Davidson Institute for Talent Development
http://www.davidsongifted.org
This site offers extensive materials and opportunities for highly gifted children and their families.

Gifted Development Center
http://www.gifteddevelopment.com
This center tests gifted students, prescribes appropriate education, and shares articles and other online resources.

National Association for Gifted Children
http://www.nagc.org
The NAGC Web site provides extensive information on advocacy, programming, and publications beneficial for teachers and parents of gifted children.

National Research Center on the Gifted and Talented (NRC/GT)
http://www.gifted.uconn.edu/nrcgt.html
The center conducts research, makes findings available online, and produces a regular newsletter, among other resources.

Supporting Emotional Needs of the Gifted (SENG)
http://www.sengifted.org
SENG provides articles and other resources for parents and educators focusing on the affective needs of gifted learners.

Uniquely Gifted
http://www.uniquelygifted.org
This is a support site for gifted students who are twice- or multiply exceptional.

Mentoring

International Telementor Program
http://www.telementor.org
Initiated in 1995, this extensive program is run by the Colorado Nonprofit Development Center and partially supported by the U.S. Department of Education. This program has assisted more than 40,000 students.

Mentor
http://www.mentoring.org
This is a comprehensive and up-to-date site for support materials and mentors.

National Mentoring Center
http://www.nwrel.org/mentoring/index.php
The Northwest Regional Educational Laboratory supports this mentoring center. Among the resources are publications, a Mentor Exchange Listserv, and a collection of FAQs and answers.

Online Communication Technologies

Microsoft Free Conferencing Software
http://www.microsoft.com
Windows Meeting Space is the version available for Windows computers running the Vista operating system; NetMeeting is for older versions. Both are conferencing software for collaboration, document sharing, and presentations.

Polycom
http://www.polycom.com
This site features a relatively inexpensive device for point-to-point Internet conferencing and transmission classes with both audio and video signals.

Skype
http://www.skype.com
Make free phone calls and conduct real-time audio/video conferences. Participants must each have the software. This software
runs on both Mac and PC computers.

Wikispaces for Educators
http://www.wikispaces.com/site/for/teachers
The sponsoring company donates free wiki hosting for K–12
educators. Wikis allow multiple individuals to write and edit
documents together.

Wimba
http://www.wimba.com/products
This company produces several kinds of conferencing and instructional software specifically intended for educators. Training is
needed to use the powerful Collaboration Suite effectively as
a supplement for online instruction. Prices are not specified;
however, districts or consortia with limited funds might be able
to negotiate reasonable terms. Demos are available online.

Rural Education Support

McREL: Rural Education
http://www.mcrel.org/topics/RuralEducation
This site contains links to many resources on rural education.
Most resources are available for purchase to guide rural school
administrators, in addition to external links on rural schools.

National Research Center on Rural Education Support
(NRCRES)
http://www.nrcres.org
The NRCRES site says "their focus is retention of qualified teachers, student achievement and dropout, availability of and access to
opportunities for advanced placement courses and improvement
in teacher quality through professional development."

National Rural Education Association (NREA)
http://www.nrea.net
This site has useful links to a wide variety of organizations from the Contact Us: Links tab.

The Rural School and Community Trust
http://www.ruraledu.org
The trust is a national nonprofit organization that focuses on connection schools have with their communities and what it takes to make both stronger. Their recent publication, *Why Rural Matters 2007: The Realities of Rural Education Growth*, is a "must read" for understanding critical issues facing rural schools.

References

Arnold, M. L., Biscoe, B., Farmer, T. W., Robertson, D. L., & Shapley, K. L. (2007). *How the government defines rural has implications for education policies and practices* (Issues & Answers Report, REL 2007-No.010). Washington, DC: U.S. Department of Education, Institute of Education Sciences, National Center for Education Evaluation and Regional Assistance, Regional Educational Laboratory Southwest. Retrieved June 2, 2008, from http://ies.ed.gov/ncee/edlabs

Avery, L. D., & Little, C. A. (2003). Concept development and learning. In J. VanTassel-Baska & C. A. Little (Eds.), *Content-based curriculum for high-ability learners* (pp. 101–124). Waco, TX: Prufrock Press.

Azzam, A. H. (2007/2008). Left behind—by design. *Educational Leadership, 65*(4), 91–92.

Belcastro, F. P. (2002). Electronic technology and its use with rural gifted students. *Roeper Review, 25,* 14–16.

Birch, J. W. (2004). Is *any* identification procedure necessary? In J. S. Renzulli (Ed.), *Identification of students for gifted and talented programs* (pp. 1–10). Thousand Oaks, CA: Corwin Press.

Borland, J. H. (1989). *Planning and implementing programs for the gifted*. New York: Teachers College Press.

Clark, B. (2008). *Growing up gifted: Developing the potential of children at home and at school* (7th ed.). Upper Saddle River, NJ: Pearson.

Clark, L. (2005). Gifted and growing. *Educational Leadership, 63*(3), 56–60.

Clasen, D. R., & Clasen, R. E. (2003). Mentoring the gifted and talented. In N. Colangelo & G. A. Davis (Eds.), *Handbook of gifted education* (3rd ed., pp. 254–267). Boston: Allyn & Bacon.

Colangelo, N., Assouline, S. G., & Gross, M. U. M. (2004). *A nation deceived: How schools hold back America's brightest students* (Vol. 1). Iowa City: The University of Iowa, The Connie Belin & Jacqueline N. Blank International Center for Gifted Education and Talent Development.

Colangelo, N., Assouline, S. G., & New, J. K. (1999). *Gifted education in rural schools: A national assessment*. Iowa City: The University of Iowa, The Connie Belin & Jacqueline N. Blank International Center for Gifted Education and Talent Development.

Colangelo, N., Assouline, S. G., & New, J. K. (2001). *Gifted voices from rural America*. Iowa City: The University of Iowa, The Connie Belin & Jacqueline N. Blank International Center for Gifted Education and Talent Development.

Colangelo, N., & Davis, G. A. (Eds.). (2003). *Handbook of gifted education* (3rd ed.). Boston: Allyn & Bacon.

Davis, G. A., & Rimm, S. B. (2004). *Education of the gifted and talented* (5th ed.). Boston: Simon & Schuster.

Delisle, J., & Lewis, B. A. (2003). *The survival guide for teachers of gifted kids: How to plan, manage, and evaluate programs for gifted youth K–12*. Minneapolis, MN: Free Spirit.

Dodge, B. (1995). *Some thoughts about WebQuests*. Retrieved July 23, 2008, from http://webquest.sdsu.edu/about_webquests.html

Friend, M. (2008). *Special education: Contemporary perspectives for school professionals* (2nd ed.). Boston: Pearson.

Gentry, M. (2006). No Child Left Behind: Neglecting excellence. *Roeper Review, 29,* 24–27.

Gross, M. U. M. (2002). "Play partner" or "sure shelter": What gifted children look for in friendship. *SENG Newsletter, 2*(2), 1–3. Retrieved July 23, 2008, from http://www.sengifted. org/articles_social/Gross_PlayPartnerOrSureShelter.shtml

Howley, A. (2002). The progress of gifted students in a rural district that emphasized acceleration strategies. *Roeper Review, 24,* 158–160.

Howley, A., Howley, C. B., & Pendarvis, E. D. (1986). *Teaching gifted children: Principles and strategies.* Boston: Little, Brown.

Howley, C. B., Howley, A., & Pendarvis, E. D. (1995). *Out of our minds: Anti-intellectualism and talent development in American schooling.* New York: Teachers College Press.

Institute of Education Sciences (IES). (n.d.). *Navigating resources for rural schools.* Retrieved June 3, 2008, from http://nces. ed.gov/surveys/ruraled/page2.asp

Johnsen, S. K. (2004). *Identifying gifted students: A practical guide.* Waco, TX: Prufrock Press.

Johnson, J., & Strange, M. (2007). *Why rural matters 2007: The realities of rural education growth.* Arlington, VA: Rural School and Community Trust. Retrieved March 16, 2009, from http://files.ruraledu.org/wrm07/WRM07.pdf

Karnes, F. A., & Stephens, K. R. (2000). *The ultimate guide for student product development & evaluation.* Waco, TX: Prufrock Press.

Karnes, F. A., & Stephens, K. R. (2008). *Achieving excellence educating the gifted and talented.* Upper Saddle River, NJ: Pearson.

Kulik, J. A. (1992). *An analysis of the research on ability grouping: Historical and contemporary perspectives* (RBDM 9204). Storrs: University of Connecticut, National Research Center on the Gifted and Talented.

Lewis, J. D., & Clark, B. I. (2003, February). *WebQuest: Collaborative problem solving using the Web.* Presentation at the annual convention of the Nebraska Association for the Gifted, Lincoln, NE.

Lewis, J. D., Cruzeiro, P. A., & Hall, C. A. (2007). Impact of two elementary principals' leadership on gifted education in their buildings. *Gifted Child Today, 30*(2), 56–62.

Lewis, J. D., & Hafer, C. (2007). The challenges of being gifted in a rural community. *Duke Gifted Letter, 7*(2). Retrieved January 31, 2007, from http://www.dukegiftedletter.com/articles/vol7no2_feature.html

Little, C. A. (2003). Adapting language arts curricula for high-ability learners. In J. VanTassel-Baska & C. A. Little (Eds.), *Content-based curriculum for high-ability learners* (pp. 127–159). Waco, TX: Prufrock Press.

Luhman, A., & Fundis, R. (1989). *Building academically strong gifted programs in rural schools. ERIC Digest.* (ERIC Document Reproduction Service Number ED308060) Retrieved July 15, 2008, from http://www.nagc.org/index.aspx?id=179

Maker, C. J., & Nielson, A. B. (1996). *Teaching models in education of the gifted* (2nd ed.). Austin, TX: Pro-Ed.

Manning, S., & Besnoy, K. D. (2008). *Special populations.* In F. A. Karnes & S. R. Stephens (Eds.), *Achieving excellence: Educating the gifted and talented* (pp. 116–134). Upper Saddle River, NJ: Merrill/Prentice Hall.

Mendozo, C. (2006). Inside today's classrooms: Teacher voices on No Child Left Behind and the education of gifted children. *Roeper Review, 29,* 28–31.

National Association for Gifted Children. (1998). *Pre-K–grade 12 gifted program standards.* Retrieved from http://www.nagc.org/uploadedFiles/PDF/Standards_PDFs/k12%20GT%20standards%20brochure.pdf

National Education Association. (n.d.). *Rural schools: Background.* Retrieved March 2, 2009, from http://www.nea.org/home/20412.htm

National Research Center on Rural Education Support. (2005). *Mission.* Retrieved June 23, 2008, from http://www.nrcres.org

Reis, S. M., & Renzulli, J. S. (1982). *A case for a broadened conception of giftedness.* Retrieved June 25, 2008, from http://www.gifted.uconn.edu/sem/pdf/Broadened_Conception_Giftedness.pdf

Reis, S. M., Westberg, K. L., Kulikowich, J., Caillard, F., Hébert, T., Plucker, J., et al. (1993). *Why not let high ability students start school in January? The curriculum compacting study* (Research Monograph 93106). Storrs: University of Connecticut, National Research Center on the Gifted and Talented. Retrieved June 25, 2008, from http://www.gifted.uconn.edu/nrcgt/reports/rm93106/rm93106.pdf

Roberts, J. L., & Inman, T. F. (2007). *Strategies for differentiating instruction: Best practices for the classroom.* Waco, TX: Prufrock Press.

Robinson, A., Shore, B. M., & Enersen, D. L. (2007). *Best practices in gifted education: An evidence-based guide.* Waco, TX: Prufrock Press.

Rogers, K. B. (1991). *The relationship of grouping practices to the education of the gifted and talented learner* (RBDM 9102). Storrs: University of Connecticut, National Research Center on the Gifted and Talented. Retrieved June 2, 2008, from http://www.gifted.uconn.edu/nrcgt/reports/rbdm9102/rbdm9102.pdf

Rogers, K. B. (2002). *Re-forming gifted education: Matching the program to the child.* Scottsdale, AZ: Great Potential Press.

Tomlinson, C. A. (1999). *The differentiated classroom: Responding to the needs of all learners.* Alexandria, VA: Association for Supervision and Curriculum Development.

VanTassel-Baska, J. (1998). *Excellence in educating gifted & talented learners.* Denver: Love.

VanTassel-Baska, J. (2003a). Content-based curriculum for high-ability learners: An introduction. In J. VanTassel-Baska & C. A. Little (Eds.), *Content-based curriculum for high-ability learners* (pp. 1–23). Waco, TX: Prufrock Press.

VanTassel-Baska, J. (2003b). *Curriculum & instructional planning & design for gifted learners.* Denver: Love.

VanTassel-Baska, J., & Stambaugh, T. (2006). *Comprehensive curriculum for gifted learners* (3rd ed.). Boston: Pearson.

Winebrenner, S. (2001). *Teaching gifted kids in the regular classroom* (Rev. ed.). Minneapolis, MN: Free Spirit.

Joan D. Lewis is professor of teacher education at the University of Nebraska at Kearney where she directs the graduate program in gifted education for the University of Nebraska system. She has published articles on a variety of topics and speaks frequently at local, state, national, and international conferences in the areas of alternative assessment, gifted girls, public relations and advocacy, rural gifted education, and uses of technology in education. Dr. Lewis' most recent research focuses on the impact school principals have on gifted education. Her work with local and state associations in gifted education has spanned more than 26 years.

Printed in the United States
by Baker & Taylor Publisher Services